D1308811

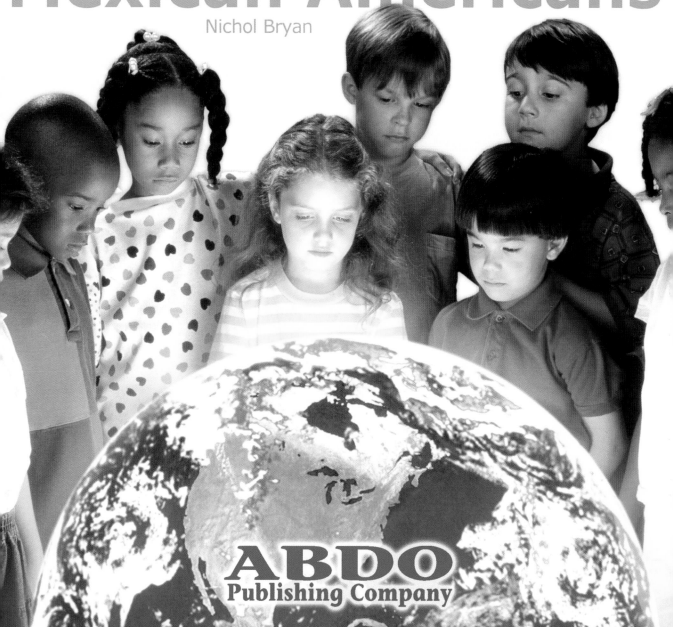

Mexican Americans

Nichol Bryan

ABDO
Publishing Company

visit us at
www.abdopub.com

Published by ABDO Publishing Company, 4940 Viking Drive, Edina, Minnesota 55435.
Copyright © 2004 by Abdo Consulting Group, Inc. International copyrights reserved in all
countries. No part of this book may be reproduced in any form without written permission from
the publisher.

Printed in the United States.

Cover Photo: Corbis
Interior Photos: AP/Wide World p. 22; Corbis pp. 1, 2-3, 4, 6, 7, 9, 10, 13, 14, 16, 19, 20, 23, 24,
    25, 27, 28, 29, 30-31; Getty Images p. 26; Kayte Deioma pp. 5, 21

Editors: Kate A. Conley, Jennifer R. Krueger, Kristin Van Cleaf
Art Direction & Maps: Neil Klinepier

All of the U.S. population statistics in the One Nation series are taken from the 2000 Census.

Library of Congress Cataloging-in-Publication Data

Bryan, Nichol, 1958-
    Mexican Americans / Nichol Bryan.
        p. cm. -- (One nation)
    Includes index.
    Summary: Provides information on the history of Mexico and on the customs, language,
religion, and experiences of Mexican Americans.
    ISBN 1-57765-987-2
    1. Mexican Americans--Juvenile literature. [1. Mexican Americans. 2. Immigrants.] I. Title.

E184.M5B765 2003
973'.046872--dc21

2002043633

Contents

Mexican Americans

Mexico and the United States are neighbors. These two countries have had a close relationship since the 1800s. In fact, Mexicans were some of the first settlers on land that is now part of the United States. Mexicans helped build America.

A Mexican-American girl dressed up for Cinco de Mayo

Despite this, Mexican Americans have not always had an easy time in America. They have worked hard while facing both **discrimination** and **prejudice**. Through it all, though, Mexican Americans have not given up. They have built strong communities and fought for their rights. They have made their own **culture** a part of American culture.

A girl dressed in a mariachi costume joins a celebration honoring the patron saint of musicians.

Mexico's Past

Indians were the first people to live in present-day Mexico. These people hunted and farmed for hundreds of years. They developed into **cultures** such as the Maya, Mixtecs, Zapotecs, and Aztecs. The Aztecs built the last great empire of Mexico in the 1400s.

Cortés meets with Montezuma II, the last emperor of the Aztecs.

Spanish explorers first landed in North and South America in the early 1500s. In 1518 Hernán Cortés, a Spanish **conquistador**, founded Mexico's first Spanish settlement, called Veracruz. By 1521, Cortés and his army had conquered the Aztecs. The Spaniards then set up a colony they called New Spain. They forced many of the Indian peoples to convert to Catholicism and to pay taxes to the Spaniards.

Between 1540 and 1542, the Spanish explorer Francisco Vásquez de Coronado explored north of New Spain. By the end of his journey, he had claimed a large area that is now the Southwestern United States. Settlers from New Spain began moving into this area in the 1600s.

The 1800s brought great changes for New Spain. In 1810, the people **rebelled** against the Spaniards, and years of conflict followed. The people finally freed themselves from Spanish rule in 1821. New Spain became the Mexican Empire.

A painting of Francisco Vásquez de Coronado exploring the Southwest

The Mexican Empire was weak and didn't last. The people drove out the emperor in 1823. They formed a **republic** with a **constitution** the next year. Meanwhile, U.S. settlers were pushing farther and farther west. By the 1830s, some 30,000 U.S. settlers lived in Texas, which was then Mexican territory.

Texans **rebelled** against Mexican rule and formed their own republic in 1836. In 1845, Texas became part of the United States. But, the United States and Mexico disagreed about Texas's southern border. This disagreement led to the Mexican War.

In 1848, the two countries signed a treaty giving most of Mexico's northern territory to the United States. Five years later, the United States purchased more land. Some people living in these areas moved south to Mexico. But, thousands more Mexicans became Americans without even trying!

The United States & Mexico in the 1800s

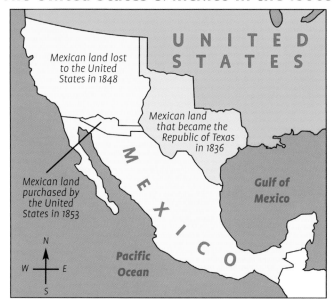

Mexican land lost to the United States in 1848

Mexican land that became the Republic of Texas in 1836

Mexican land purchased by the United States in 1853

UNITED STATES

MEXICO

Gulf of Mexico

Pacific Ocean

N
W — E
S

The Mexican War had ended, but Mexico's problems were far from over. Mexicans were upset over the American victory, and the **economy** was weak. Benito Juárez and other leaders tried to make reforms. But, the people disagreed on what changes to make. A **civil war** called the War of the Reform broke out.

In 1863, France invaded and took control of Mexico. Four years later, the Mexicans regained control of their country. In 1876, Porfirio Díaz became the country's president. Under his leadership, Mexico's economy improved. Railroads were built, and industry expanded. But, workers received low wages, and many Indians lost their land to wealthy landowners. As a result, most Mexicans were very poor, and many migrated to the United States to find work.

*President
Porfirio Díaz*

Farmers and workers took up arms to overthrow the government in 1910, beginning the Mexican Revolution. Groups led by Emiliano Zapata and Francisco "Pancho" Villa fought against the government. Thousands of Mexicans fled north to the United States. This wave of **immigration** continued into the 1930s.

Pancho Villa on his horse

In 1917, Mexico finally wrote a new **constitution**. During the 1920s, the government began many social and **economic** reforms. Then in 1928, the National Revolutionary Party, which later became the Institutional Revolutionary Party (PRI), took control of the government. It ruled Mexico for the next 70 years.

The Mexican government continued its reforms. During World War II, Mexico contributed supplies to support America's war effort. For the next 35 years, Mexico's economy continued to grow. The sale of oil discovered in the 1970s was a large part of the economy.

However, unemployment was still a problem. The problem grew worse in the 1980s, when oil prices fell, hurting the economy. Throughout these years, many Mexicans migrated north. Most entered the United States legally, looking for work. But some came illegally, hurting Mexico's friendship with the United States.

Mexico, the United States, and Canada signed the North American Free Trade Agreement (NAFTA) in 1992. NAFTA was meant to make trade easier between these three nations. Despite this, Mexico's **economic** problems continued through the 1990s.

After seven decades in power, the PRI was defeated in the 2000 election. Vicente Fox Quesada was elected president in one of the freest elections in Mexican history. Today Mexicans are hopeful, but many still live in poverty.

The Journey from Mexico to the United States

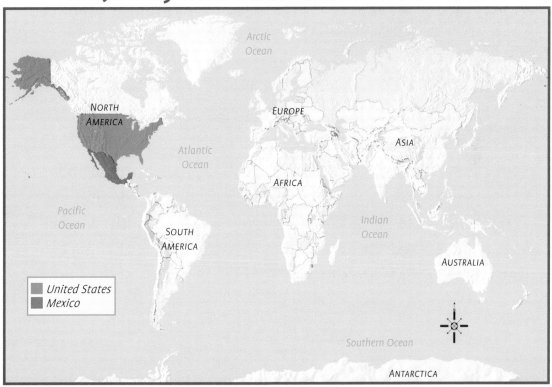

Early Americans

How did Mexican Americans get to be such a large and important group in the United States? First, they have been coming to the United States longer than other people. Second, they are neighbors. Getting here requires no costly boat or plane ticket.

The first Mexican Americans were already living in the Southwest when it became U.S. territory in 1848. Some were wealthy landowners, but most tended small farms. They slowly became the minority as more settlers came from the east, looking for mining profits.

With these eastern settlers came **prejudice**. Many of the settlers were Protestants. This made it hard for them to accept Mexican Americans, who were mostly Catholic. In addition, the eastern settlers wanted land. Though Mexican Americans had been living on their land for years, they were required to show proof of ownership. Many were cheated out of their land.

The first big wave of Mexican **immigrants** consisted of people fleeing the Mexican Revolution. Between 1910 and 1930, nearly 680,000 Mexicans moved to the United States. In these years, immigrants were a main source of labor in the American Southwest. They worked for low wages in factories and mines, or on railroads and farms. The work was sometimes dangerous, and living conditions could be terrible.

New Mexican settlers stand in front of their sod house around 1895.

In World War I, thousands of Mexican Americans volunteered to fight for the United States. Still, many Mexican Americans struggled with **discrimination**. They were often kept from better wages, jobs, and housing. To deal with this, Mexican Americans formed labor unions and went on strikes for better wages. They formed organizations to deal with social problems.

In 1924, the U.S. government established a border patrol to stop illegal **immigration**. The Mexican immigration rate slowed after this. Then in the 1930s, America's **economy** fell into a **depression**.

Living conditions for migrant workers could be poor, as can be seen by this worker's home in California in 1937.

Many people believed Mexican workers were taking jobs from other Americans. Some public places were **segregated**. Children were punished if caught speaking Spanish in school.

Mexican-American Communities

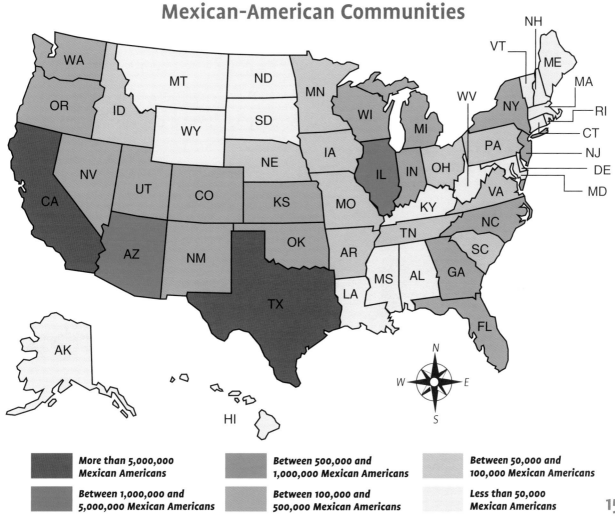

| | More than 5,000,000 Mexican Americans | | Between 500,000 and 1,000,000 Mexican Americans | | Between 50,000 and 100,000 Mexican Americans |
| | Between 1,000,000 and 5,000,000 Mexican Americans | | Between 100,000 and 500,000 Mexican Americans | | Less than 50,000 Mexican Americans |

Braceros often did "stoop" labor, bending down to pick fruits and vegetables for 10 to 12 hours a day.

The United States and Mexico formed a program to return some Mexicans to Mexico. The program was supposed to be for people who wanted to return, but it didn't work out that way. The U.S. government sent back thousands of people against their will. Some were U.S. citizens, and some had even been born in the United States.

During World War II, some 300,000 Mexican Americans served in the U.S. armed forces. At the same time, the United States started the Mexican Farm Labor Supply Program, or bracero program. It allowed Mexican laborers into the United States for seasonal work.

Employers liked braceros because they worked for low wages. But, many braceros were mistreated. In addition, they created competition for Mexican-American farm workers. Mexican Americans could not live on such low wages. So, they formed labor unions.

During the last 50 years, many more Mexican **immigrants** have come to America. The Southwestern United States is home to many Mexican-American communities. New immigrants join these communities regularly, keeping Mexican traditions alive.

Life for Mexican Americans has improved slowly. In the 1960s, the Chicano movement developed pride in Mexican-American **culture**. Today's America has more Mexican-American representation in government, and **prejudice** is lessening.

But, there are still problems. For example, most Mexican immigrants enter the United States legally. But, some slip across the border illegally. To stop this, border patrols watch for illegal immigrants. Unfortunately, it means some people think all Mexican Americans are illegal immigrants.

Today, about 21 million Americans are of Mexican descent. Of that total, more than 9 million were born in Mexico. Mexican Americans are one of the fastest-growing groups in the United States.

Becoming a Citizen

Mexicans and other **immigrants** who come to the United States take the same path to citizenship. Immigrants become citizens in a process called naturalization. A government agency called the Immigration and Naturalization Service (INS) oversees this process.

The Path to Citizenship

Applying for Citizenship

The first step in becoming a citizen is filling out a form. It is called the Application for Naturalization. On the application, immigrants provide information about their past. Immigrants send the application to the INS.

Providing Information

Besides the application, immigrants must provide the INS with other items. They may include documents such as marriage licenses or old tax returns. Immigrants must also provide photographs and fingerprints. They are used for identification. The fingerprints are also used to check whether immigrants have committed crimes in the past.

The Interview

Next, an INS officer interviews each immigrant to discuss his or her application and background. In addition, the INS officer tests the immigrant's ability to speak, read, and write in English. The officer also tests the immigrant's knowledge of American civics.

The Oath

Immigrants approved for citizenship must take the Oath of Allegiance. Once immigrants take this oath, they are citizens. During the oath, immigrants promise to renounce loyalty to their native country, to support the U.S. Constitution, and to serve and defend the United States when needed.

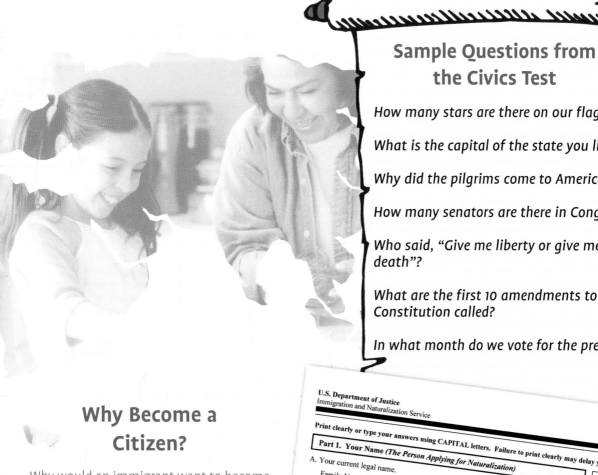

Sample Questions from the Civics Test

How many stars are there on our flag?

What is the capital of the state you live in?

Why did the pilgrims come to America?

How many senators are there in Congress?

Who said, "Give me liberty or give me death"?

What are the first 10 amendments to the Constitution called?

In what month do we vote for the president?

Why Become a Citizen?

Why would an immigrant want to become a U.S. citizen? There are many reasons. Perhaps the biggest reason is that the U.S. Constitution grants many rights to its citizens. One of the most important is the right to vote.

U.S. Department of Justice
Immigration and Naturalization Service

Print clearly or type your answers using CAPITAL letters. Failure to print clearly may delay your application. Use bla

Application f

Part 1. Your Name *(The Person Applying for Naturalization)*

A. Your current legal name.

Family Name *(Last Name)*

Write your INS "A"- n
A _ _ _ _ _

Given Name *(First Name)*

Full Middle Name *(If applicable)*

FOR INS US

Bar Code

B. Your name exactly as it appears on your Permanent Resident Card.

Family Name *(Last Name)*

Given Name *(First Name)*

Full Middle Name *(If applicable)*

C. If you have ever used other names, provide them below.

Family Name *(Last Name)*

Given Name *(First Name)*

Middle Name

Life in America

Mexican traditions are a large part of Mexican-American life. Mexican-American families, as well as recent **immigrants**, keep these traditions alive. The longer a family lives in the United States, the more its members lose some traditional Mexican beliefs and attitudes. However, they often create a blend of **cultures** that is **uniquely** Mexican-American.

La Familia

Family, or *la familia*, is a central part of Mexican-American life. For Mexican Americans, family is more than just parents, brothers, and sisters. It includes uncles, aunts, cousins, grandparents, godparents, and even close friends.

A Mexican-American father and son

Traditionally, the father was the authority in a Mexican family. Mothers cared for the children and home. However, Mexican-American homes are changing. Mothers often need to work outside the home to earn money for the family. Fathers have a larger role in the home than they used to. Still, Mexican Americans are close to their family members. They often help recent **immigrants** learn about life in America.

Fiestas

Fiestas are also a part of Mexican-American **culture**. Fiestas often include the music of mariachis, or bands of Mexican musicians. Piñatas, paper flowers, and *cascarónes* often decorate these celebrations.

Mexico celebrates its independence on September 16. Mexican Americans join this celebration with music and dancing. The green, white, and red Mexican flag is seen everywhere at this fiesta. One of the day's main

Mariachi musicians play together at the Fiesta de Santa Cecilia in Los Angeles.

dishes, *chiles en nogada*, has ingredients that are the same colors as the flag! During the celebration, the people gather to shout "Viva Mexico!" and light fireworks.

Cinco de Mayo, which means the Fifth of May, is a fiesta well known in the United States. This marks the day in 1862 when the Mexicans won a battle against the French. This holiday has become popular with all Americans.

In the fall comes the Day of the Dead, which is when Mexicans honor relatives who have died. People set out pictures of their loved ones along with things they liked. Candy skulls and sweet bread are also a part of the celebration.

A girl paints her face to look like a candy skull for Día de los Muertos, or Day of the Dead.

Food

What is your favorite Mexican food? Tacos? Burritos? Tamales? Mexican-American **culture** brings foods such as rice, beans, corn tortillas, chiles, and sauces to the United States. Mexican restaurants are popular in many U.S. cities. While some dishes have become Americanized, they still carry the flavor of Mexico.

Many Americans are familiar with Mexican enchiladas, burritos, rice, and refried beans.

23

A Roman Catholic People

Mexico's people are mainly Roman Catholic. So, it is no surprise that a large number of Mexican Americans are also Catholic. The **Virgin Mary** is special to Mexican and Mexican-American Catholics. To many, she is known as Our Lady of Guadalupe.

According to legend, in 1531 a man named Juan Diego had a vision of the Virgin Mary while standing on a hill called Tepeyac. After Diego's vision, roses miraculously appeared on the hill. In addition, an image of Mary also appeared on Diego's cloak. The people built a church on Tepeyac. The Virgin of Guadalupe's image is still found in many Mexican and Mexican-American homes.

The San José de Tumacácori mission in Arizona was constructed in 1691 by Catholics from New Spain.

America's Second Language

Mexican Americans brought with them not only their **culture** but also their language, Spanish. It is America's second-most commonly spoken language. In fact, there are many U.S. neighborhoods where Spanish is the main language spoken.

States such as Texas, California, and New Mexico have many Spanish-language newspapers, radio stations, and television stations. In many large Mexican-American communities, schools offer classes in both Spanish and English. These classes help Spanish-speaking students keep up in school while they learn English.

In places such as California, many students are taught in both English and Spanish.

However, not all Mexican Americans speak Spanish, or only Spanish. The longer a Mexican-American family has lived in the United States, the more likely its members are to speak English. For many second-, third-, and fourth-generation Mexican Americans, English is their main language.

25

Giving Back

The history of Mexicans in America is a struggle for rights and respect. Today, Mexican Americans have many more opportunities open to them than in the past. Some are scientists, such as Mario Molina, who in 1995 won the **Nobel Prize** in chemistry for his study of the ozone layer. Others are astronauts, such as Ellen Ochoa. She was the first Mexican-American woman to become an astronaut, and to go into space. She has flown on several space shuttle missions.

One of the people who led the labor struggle that created these opportunities was Cesar Chavez. He was a labor union organizer and spokesperson for the poor, especially for his fellow Mexican-American farm workers.

Ellen Ochoa holds her son after returning from a shuttle mission.

In 1962, Chavez formed what later became the United Farm Workers of America. The organization helps migrant workers in California receive better working conditions. Chavez urged workers not to use violence as a way to get what they wanted.

As the Mexican-American community grew and became better organized, its people were able to elect their own members to public office. Octaviano Larrazolo, a Mexican **immigrant**, did much to protect the rights of Spanish speakers in New Mexico. He was the state's governor from 1918 to 1922. In 1928, he became the first Mexican-American senator.

Cesar Chavez

Larrazolo paved the way for other Mexican-American lawmakers. For example, in 1993 Lucille Roybal-Allard became the first Mexican-American woman elected to the House of Representatives. She still works hard to improve opportunities for the people of her district in California.

Mexican-American talents are also a part of American arts. Marta Sanchez paints on metal, with themes inspired by traditional Mexican arts. Her best-known works are *retablo* paintings, a type of prayer painting that often tells a story. Her paintings have been exhibited around the United States and Mexico.

Mexican Americans contribute to the world of sports, too. If you like baseball, you already know about Fernando Valenzuela. He was born in Mexico, and when he joined the Los Angeles Dodgers in

1980 he could barely speak English. But, he developed a pitch that was one of the most unhittable in baseball. In 1981, the popular Valenzuela was the first baseball player to receive both the National League Rookie of the Year Award and the Cy Young Award in the same year.

Mexican Americans have also had a big influence on American music. The band Los Lobos has become popular even with non-Spanish speaking

Fernando Valenzuela gives an interview.

listeners. Some people call their style of music Tex-Mex, a form of rock music with a Latin sound. *Good Morning Aztlán*, their latest album, was released in 2002.

The legendary Carlos Santana has captured audiences ever since his father taught him mariachi music nearly 50 years ago. In the 1960s, Santana introduced Americans to his special Latin sound with hit songs such as "Oye Como Va" and "Black Magic Woman." His music has earned him many honors, including a place in the Rock and Roll Hall of Fame and several Grammy Awards.

Mexican Americans have worked and fought hard for what they have. And, they continue to make their mark on American life. More and more, Mexican **culture** is becoming part of the culture of every American.

Carlos Santana

Glossary

cascarónes - hollowed-out eggshells that have been painted and filled with confetti.

civil war - a war between groups in the same country.

conquistador - a leader in the Spanish conquest of the Americas.

constitution - the laws that govern a country.

culture - the customs, arts, and tools of a nation or people at a certain time.

depression - a period of economic trouble when there is little buying or selling and many people are out of work.

discrimination - unfair treatment based on factors such as a person's race, religion, or gender.

economy - the way a nation uses its money, goods, and natural resources.

immigration - entry into another country to live. People who immigrate are called immigrants.

Nobel Prize - an award given to someone who has made outstanding achievements in his or her field of study.

prejudice - hatred of a particular group based on factors such as race or religion.

rebel - to disobey an authority or the government.

republic - a form of government in which authority rests with voting citizens and is carried out by elected officials, such as those in a parliament.

segregation - the separation or isolation of a race, class, or ethnic group from a dominant group.

unique - being the only one of its kind.

Virgin Mary - the mother of Jesus.

Saying It

Benito Juárez - beh-NEE-toh WAHR-uhs
braceros - brah-SEHR-ohs
cascarónes - kahs-kah-ROHN-ays
Cesar Chavez - SAY-sahr CHAH-vays
chiles en nogada - CHEE-lays ehn no-GAH-dah
conquistador - kahn-KEES-tuh-dawr
Fernando Valenzuela - fehr-NAHN-doh vahl-ehn-ZWAY-lah
Hernán Cortés - ehr-NAHN kawr-TAYS
la familia - LAH fah-MEEL-yah
Octaviano Larrazolo - awk-tah-VYAH-noh lah-rah-SOH-loh
Vicente Fox Quesada - vee-SEHN-tay FAWKS kay-SAH-dah

Web Sites

To learn more about Mexican Americans, visit ABDO Publishing Company on the World Wide Web at **www.abdopub.com**. Web sites about Mexican Americans are featured on our Book Links page. These links are routinely monitored and updated to provide the most current information available.

Index